THE UNKNOWN JOURNEY OF MY LIFE

DELANO J. SAMUELS

Published by: Divine Book Design & Consultants
Website: divinebookdesign.com

CONTENTS

DEDICATION

"**The Unknown Journey of My Life**" is dedicated to everyone. It is written to encourage, edify, and empower anyone who believes their life seems meaningless.

If you feel that you have no hope for a better tomorrow because of what people have spoken or are discouraged about your position in life, this book is for you. Your current position in life might be misleading to you and others but not God.

Are you wondering if the Lord Jesus Christ cares? I want to tell you **"YES."** The Lord cares; you can have a "better tomorrow" no matter what life throws at you. Never give up because '**greatness**' is in you.

Jeremiah 29:11- ***'For I know the thoughts that I think toward you, saith the Lord, thoughts of peace, and not of evil, to give you an expected end.'***

ACKNOWLEDGEMENT

First, I would like to acknowledge the Holy Spirit. Without His guidance and knowledge, this book would not be possible.

God also sent some amazing and wonderful helpers into my life, and they played an awesome role when I felt helpless. They became paramount important vessels to assist me in crossing over from my yesterday into my today.

Paul McKenzie, Clayton McGhie, Carol Graham, Darcus Watson, Eula Frazer, and Everton Stewart. I love you all.

I also want to thank Andrea Douglas for her review and ideas. God bless you richly.

1
THE START OF MY LIFE

"Every thief is a liar, and every liar is a thief." These were Agatha Hunter's favourite words to me. She was my grandmother, but also my mother. It all began on a little island called Jamaica. When I was three months old, my biological parents, Marcia Samuels and Jeffrey Samuels, took me to my grandmother to be raised by her. Hard and troubling times were upon them, so they made the best decision for themselves and me.

Being the first son of my father and the first grandson of my father's parents, I was taken to reside with my grandparents in the country. Agatha Hunter and Roy Hunter cared for me, and I thank God for them. It was one of the best decisions that my parents could have ever made. The love of God will always, at any time, cause someone, somewhere, somehow to become a blessing to you, and that was what happened to me, which can also happen to you.

***"For the Lord is good; His mercy is everlasting, and His truth endureth to all generations."* Psalm 100: 5**

A few years later, my parents came to reside in my grandparents' district, Savannah Cross, Clarendon. Growing up with my brothers, sisters, and cousins in my community felt wonderful. Having them and my family in my life meant a lot to me.

"A new commandment I give unto you, that ye love one another; as I have loved you, that ye also love one another." John 13: 34.

All those long years taken from me when my parents were not around, having them return to my life was a great blessing. I began to understand the concept of LOVE and what God meant in His word about honouring and loving your parents.

Forgiveness is also critical, and it is something that is needed in everyone's life. From an early age, I began understanding what God said and meant in His word from Matthew 19: 19 and Ephesians 6: 1-2.

My parents encountered a lot of challenging times. I remember the devastating, struggling days I lived with them in the Bushy Park community of Clarendon. My father was a machine operator at the Bushy Park Bag Factory. He would be overworked, tired, and impoverished, but he would earnestly sacrifice the little he and my mother earned to stretch the finances to pay rent and make provisions for all their children. It was one of many stressful years of fighting through the hardships of life.

One thing was for certain: no matter how low things were, my parents always ensured that their children had something to eat, even if it was just a slice of bread with butter and a cup of lemonade. The quality of our lifestyle was low, but being imperfect beings, my parents would ensure shelter was over our heads.

Parents are truly a blessing from the Lord, and as children, we do not always know how much our parents care for us by making great sacrifices to make provision for us.

It does not matter who you are or where you are from; "LOVE" is one of the greatest things we must have for each other in this world and our lifetime. Remember, God is love, and everyone needs to be loved, for it is the Lord's will.

Over the years, I have learned that it is our responsibility as children to always respect our parents. It doesn't matter how grown you have become or where you are spiritually, financially, or physically. Once you have parents, the onus is on you to have and show them respect in the sight of God. I know that sometimes they can be hard on us, but the truth is, they do love us.

So, as we show respect and honour them, let us pray unto God for His help in being the best children we can be to them.

"Casting all your care upon him; for he careth for you."1 Peter 5: 7

Growing up, I had to go to church almost every Sunday with my family. I would sleep the entire service rather than listen to the Word of God because the only thing on my mind was going home. At that time, I did not know the importance of assembling with the saints and hearing the Word of God in my life.

"When I was a child, I spoke as a child, I understood as a child, I thought as a child; but when I became a man, I put away childish things." 1 Corinthians 13: 11

I was just a child who spoke and understood as a child, and I wanted to do my own thing. It is one thing to think you are right when truly you are wrong. We often discover later that our parents were right in sending us to Church.

"Train up a child in the way he should go, and when he is old, he will not depart from it." Proverbs 22: 6

Today, I thank God for how my parents and grandparents raised me and for sending me to church, even when I did not want to go. I can truly say that it helped to shape me into the person I am today.

Becoming a teenager was a journey all by itself. I stayed home with my uncle on Saturdays until my grandmother returned from the market. This was a perfect time for my uncle to abuse me. He would use his hands to slap me continuously on my head. Each time he beat me, he would hurl nasty verbal assaults at me. His favourites were 'Ugly Boy Move from Yah Suh' and 'Ugly Bwoy Yu fava Monkey. '

'Ugly Bwoy' was my uncle's nickname for me. He made it his duty to abuse me verbally and physically. This 'ugly Bwoy' did not know God's purpose in his life.

This period of mistreatment in my life not only made me feel rejected, unloved, sad, mistreated, battered, and assaulted, but it opened a spiritual portal of 'Rejection' in my life. I became so angry, arrogant, and ignorant. I could not express what was happening to me. All I knew was that I was hurting emotionally.

Thoughts of running away lingered tirelessly in my mind. Eventually, I started to pack my bags on weekends and leave home to spend time at a friend's house to escape the 'weekend abuse'. They soon began to call me, 'walkabout Lano. '

Mama became mad as hell when she discovered that my uncle was abusing me. She told him immediately to stop beating 'Lano'. Saturdays became my dreaded fear whenever I knew Mama was going to the market.

When you have a God-given purpose to do God's will, know that the Devil will try to stop you. He will even try to use a family member, a friend or even your spouse once they allow themselves to be utilized as a vessel of dishonour for the devil.

The enemy's intent is for you not to fulfil that purpose God has placed in you. The devil cannot kill purpose; only you can defeat yourself and kill your purpose. That is why the Word of God states in John 10:10 - ***"The thief cometh not, but for to steal, and to kill,***

and to destroy. I have come that they might have life and have it more abundantly."

The Devil always forgets one thing: he is not the GREAT CREATOR. He is not GOD. What God spoke over my life was paramount to my survival.

"For I know the thoughts that I think toward you, saith the Lord, thoughts of peace, and not of evil, to give you an expected end." Jeremiah 29: 11

The abuse by my uncle continued, even after being talked to and warned by Mama not to touch me. My Uncle was determined to make my life a living hell.
Brother Anansi puts it well when he says, 'Two trouble, betta than one.'

One faithful Easter holiday, things took a turn. Mama took us to a beach where she cooked and sold. Mama's food always 'tun up'; you could smell it from afar *(Very Tasty).*
My grandmother loved going to the beach to sell fried chicken. Easter was the time of the year when she made a lot of money. We all

went with her to enjoy the scenery and swim in the seawater. My uncle was also there, and I vividly remember him hitting me for no apparent reason. I burst into tears crying.

Mama was selling chicken, but she saw what had happened. She was livid! Rage stood up in her like a monster. She threw a long fork she was using to fry her chicken at my uncle, lodging it in his back. I saw my uncle on the ground, and in a split second, death flashed before my eyes. Immediately, we all had to rush him to a nearby hospital, where he was treated and sent home.

Mama did not go to jail. No charges were made against her for hurting Uncle B. Uncle B lied to the police, saying that he fell on a wire at the beach. After that incident, the relationship with my grandmother and uncle was not the same. That continued for a very good while. Grandpa was also very upset with Mama, but after all was said and done, he turned around to agree that Uncle B was wrong in abusing me senselessly. Over time, I watched their relationship mending. ***Thank God for His grace.***

The Bible says, 'Be angry, but sin not.' Being angry for the wrong purpose can be very serious and detrimental to others, even those you love. When enraged, think before you act and weigh your words before speaking. Words are seeds, so we must be careful with the words that we say to each other. The enemy intends us to be angry and spew negative words at each other. Always remember that words have power!
"Death and life are in the power of the tongue: and they that love it shall eat the fruit thereof." Proverbs 18: 21.

The word of God is evident and true when it says, "A soft answer turneth away wrath: but grievous words stir up anger." Proverbs 15.

" Remind them to be submissive to rulers and authorities, to be obedient, to be ready for every good work, [2] to speak evil of no one, to avoid quarrelling, to be gentle, and to show perfect courtesy toward all people.." Titus 3: 1 – 2

****

Growing up, my grandmother felt no one loved me, which weighed heavily on her. I was given to her by my parents, and to make matters worse, my uncle constantly abused me. I, too, felt that way.

When you have been hurt in the past, it takes the God in you to show love to family, friends, and enemies, knowing that they hurt you while growing up. However, this is what we are commanded to do. To truly be a disciple of Jesus, we must love one another. Not only that, but we must also love our enemies as ourselves.

1 John 4: 11, 20 - "Beloved, if God so loved us, we ought also to love one another. If a man says, I love God and hateth his brother, he is a liar: for he that loveth not his brother whom he hath seen, how can he love God whom he hath not seen?"

I want to reiterate that forgiveness is very important. It is not for those who have hurt us but for those who have been hurt. We all need it to set us free and enhance us going forward. I had to do a lot of forgiving to set myself free from hurt, scars in my mind and heart, and rejection. I implore someone today to forgive so you can be free!

My High School Years

Years of frustration, coupled with abuse and rejection, spun my life into a whirlwind of struggles, and my teenage years were just the beginning of it all.

I began attending Central High School in the Parish of Clarendon, and the first day of school was crucial. I felt good seeing the teachers placing us in the right classes. My first form class was 7C. This school was supposed to start a new beginning for me. However, it was an interesting start. Deep down, I was battling anger and did not know, and that began to manifest through fighting. Immediately after being placed in my class, I fought with another boy over a bench. This was one of the most foolish things that I have ever done. The teacher was standing in the class, but luckily, she did not take us to the principal's office when she saw us fighting. Instead, she took us to the 'book room', questioned us and told us to apologize to each other. We did, shook hands, and then went back to our class.

"Trust in the Lord with all thine heart, and lean not unto thine own understanding. In all thy ways acknowledge him, and he shall direct thy paths." Proverbs 3: 5 - 6

When we do not have a relationship with God, we tend to lean on our own understanding and in doing so, mishaps will occur. This is one of the problems that lead to relationship issues, bad financial decisions, violence, and much more.

In 2001, I joined the track and field team at school and began a short but prominent track and field career. I started to embark on a vast journey across Jamaica with other athletes. One day, I became dumbstricken when I saw a girl who attended my school. I developed an instantaneous liking. I believed I had met my one true love. My emotions skyrocketed, and I could not understand what was happening to me. I began questioning myself. I wondered how young I was and if I felt this feeling was love.

"Tell me, O thou whom my soul loveth, where thou feedest, where thou makest thy flock to rest at noon: for why should I be as one that turneth aside by the flocks of thy companions?" Solomon 1: 7

Time passed, and the young lady and I started dating. I began to play the role of husband in our relationship, putting my entire heart into it. I did not stop to think of the things that could happen with falling in love at such a tender age. I am not trying to make you afraid of falling in love. Once you find that special person who, with the help of the Lord, becomes your wife or husband, it is beautiful. But remember to do so with understanding.

"I have compared thee, O my love, to a company of horses in Pharaoh's chariots. Thy cheeks are comely with rows of jewels, thy neck with chains of gold." Solomon 1: 9-10

In marriage, "agreement" is very important. It allows couples to be on the same page and be at peace with themselves. Agreement generates power, with the ability to connect and accomplish anything. It is two hands coming together to make a great sound.

"Can two walk together, except they are agreed?" Amos 3: 3

Let us stop to ask questions. Do we really love someone when we say we do, or is it that we are captivated by the person's physical appearance, how they dress, where they work, live or even how they speak? Back then, I was head over heels for the girl I met. But was this love?

We must be careful of what connects us to someone that may cause us to think and say that we love them. We must make it our duty to submit to God's direction in all we do and not be led by mere emotions and that tingling feeling we sometimes encounter when we meet someone (Butterflies).

"In all thy ways acknowledge Him, and he shall direct thy paths." Proverbs 3: 6.

Is Love Truly Blind?

We know that the word "LOVE' is one of the most four-letter words that we misuse. One must understand that there are four types of love which are:

- Storge -Family Love
- Philia - Friend bond
- Eros – Romantic love
- Agape- Unconditional "God" love

As we look at the types of love, I would love it if all men were effective by the "help" of the Holy Spirit in "Agape" love. That love makes the other three types of love come easy when necessary. Agape love is God's unconditional love. It should be the foundation of one's heart and love for others.

***

The girl I was in love with, one can only say that everything that seemed right started to turn out wrong. As our relationship continued, I encountered some very hard times with her. I did not give up and tried to be strong, even though I knew it was hard to deal with.

I began to wonder what was happening to me. To make it even more frightening, it was not the first time I had a girlfriend, but it was the first time I had true, deep feelings for a girl, and to make it so wonderful, we were going to the same school.

As youths, these things can and do happen. If I were to speak to my younger self, I would recommend focusing on education and schoolwork and getting as much out of it as possible. Trying to accomplish something tomorrow is unnecessary if it can be achieved today.

I make this appeal to every young man and young woman. If you are in a single-parent home, and your parents are trying to help you to have an education, but you are caught between choosing an education or having a relationship, "please" let it be an education. Education is the **golden key** in life, for any stage in your future and destiny. It is critical in any relationship and any stage of your life.

"Happy is the man that findeth wisdom, and the man that getteth understanding. For the

merchandise of it is better than the merchandise of silver, and the gain thereof than fine gold". Proverbs 3: 13 – 14.

Nevertheless, the best relationship to have is with the Lord Jesus Christ! He will guide you always in the right direction for your life.

My Love For Track & Field

I participated actively in school activities, and my favourite sport was Track and Field. One school sports day, I was selcted to run the 800-meter race and to be a representative for my school's 'house'. To my surprise and everyone's surprise, I became the winner, from amongst the school's track stars.

Being a winner of the school's event transformed my life overnight. In the year 2001, I was asked to become a member of the school's track and field team. However, it was a late start in preparation for my track and field career. Hence, I lacked a lot of experience. However, as time went by, I began to learn more.

In 2002, my school's team was selected among other schools to represent Jamaica at the Penns Relays. It meant an opportunity to go overseas, precisely, the United States of America. Better yet, it was a chance to travel to receive a United States Visa.

On the day of going to the embassy for the United States Visa, my coach and I had no prior preparation or communication. I was not told what to say or what to expect when I was interviewed.

Pity me, one would say. When I got to the counter, the interviewer asked me one simple, straightforward question; "What is your timing in running the 800 meters." Silly me, I replied, "52 seconds." With astonishment, he LOOKED at me with a dazed, compounding, and astounding stare and said, "WHAT!" So, he asked me again. In return, I replied, "52 minutes." By this time, the interviewer saw I had no knowledge or understanding of the sporting event I was entering. It was an instantaneous refusal of the visa. I could only attribute this to a lack of knowledge and poor communication between the coach and myself.

I have learned that whatever we do, it is best first to get the right type of understanding (God's way), "not" just our understanding.

Life Goes On

After leaving High School in 2003, I joined the Jamalco Sports Club in Clarendon, doing what I thought I loved. I never knew God's will for my life, and I was not thinking about that; I was living.

Sometimes in life, we end up doing things that have nothing to do with the will of God. Often, our feelings and emotions will lead us in the wrong direction. When the Spirit of God does not lead us, it usually causes us to miss out on our seasons of healing and breakthrough. What we think will work for us may not always be the case. Sometimes, they are just lessons to learn from.

The steps of a good man are ordered by the Lord, and he delighteth in his way.

Track & field did not work out for me, so after leaving Jamalco Sports Club, I got a job at a supermarket in May Pen Clarendon called Shopper's Fair. I started working because my grandmother could no longer support me financially. She often said, "Lano, I am giving you what I do not have."

Once I started working, I planned to send myself to evening classes to further my education. When I was in High School, I never got an opportunity to do my CXC (Caribbean Examination Council) because of financial constraints.

Along my journey, I have learned that if you have failed in some areas of your life, do not give up! Remember, ***once there is life, there is hope, and once there is hope, we can try again***. With faith in God, you will make it.

Mark 11:22 - And Jesus answering saith unto them, Have faith in God.

In those days, livestock (chickens, pigs, and goats) was what my grandmother raised to help me while playing her part as a good wife and supporting her husband. That sometimes involved planting vegetables to sell at the market and buying and selling clothes. She did anything that it took to make ends meet. It was not easy, BUT GOD!

I thank the Lord for her always for not giving up on me, even in hard times.

*****

As I continued working at the supermarket, I got so busy that I had no time to attend evening classes. All my time was taken up at work and with my ex-girlfriend, who mysteriously came back into my life. This was meant to be a distraction. My focus shifted from the dreams and plans I laid out to accomplish; not just that, but I lost my job. I wondered to myself, 'Can this be real!'

Sometimes, when you decide to go forward with your life or dreams, things will happen for you to lose focus. However, that is the time you will need to be firm and determined to reach your goals. It would be best to tell yourself you will make it, no matter the opposition.

We must be careful of what we do because one wrong move can cause many bad things to happen, even to the point where it can affect loved ones or those you care for. When you have a goal, you must be careful of your association, friends, and the voices you listen to. Not every group, friend or voice is positive. Not everyone telling you they love or care for you means what they say. They will tell you what they think you want to hear, but for sure, it is not from the goodness of their heart.

John 13:34
A new commandment I give to you, that you love one another, even as I have loved you, that you also love one another.

1 John 4:8
The one who does not love does not know God, for God is love.

Nugget

Never hurt yourself when you are going through pain caused by someone else; that individual does not know your value and worth. Be strong and move on by trusting

God. Understand that you are valuable and the apple of God's eye.

Psalm 37:23 - *The steps of a good man are ordered by the Lord: and he delighteth in his way.*

Remember I mentioned that I was out of a job? My mind started to idle on many things, staying at home where there was nothing to do but watch a movie. We had a satellite dish, so I watched anything I wanted. Pornographic movies were my choice. Being alone at home, I did not know the danger I was putting myself into. That decision affected my mentality later in life. Without understanding, I kept watching this thing.

Proverbs 30:17 - The eye is the window to the soul.

I never knew I was opening doors for sexual demons to enter my life. I started going to the strip club, which we call in Jamaica (go, go club.) I was going down the wrong path, and before I knew it, I became addicted to women. All I could think of was sex and having different women to try out different styles I premeditated.

Everything seemed good to me, and I was doing my thing. I was telling myself, "*Man, a gallist", which means* (*player*) I was indulging in sex with up to six girls at once. I could look for anyone I wanted whenever I wanted.

I can recall battling with sexual thoughts and wild imaginations from as early as my school years. I often watched a lot of horror movies, and that caused me to be very fearful, especially in my room at night when I should be sleeping. Usually, I would scream in the middle of the night. My grandmother sometimes had to get up and plead the blood of Jesus over me for me to go to sleep. ***Since then, I have had to pray every night to be able to sleep.***

I would also think of things that caused me to be mentally traumatized. I would imagine robbing and even killing. However, deep in my heart, it was not my desire to do so. The enemy injected these thoughts into my mind, and I did not know how to break free. The thoughts got so intense that I wished I could open my head and remove the thoughts plaguing my mind.

In life, we must be careful of the movies we allow our children to watch, the company they keep, and the places we allow them to go. As parents, our children often look good into our eyes because we think we are giving them everything they need to be happy. However, mentally, emotionally, and spiritually, they are in trouble because they have been exposed to things that seemed okay but were disguised by the enemy to attack their minds. Many persons entertain negative spirits by watching, reading and listening to the wrong things. For me, it was what I watched that opened the door to the spirit of fear and sexual immorality.

I thank God for a praying grandmother and all the other persons He assigned to pray for me. Yes! I believe it was prayer that kept me from going to a dark place of becoming a gunman.

It is hard when you do not know better or do not associate yourself with peers who will lead you on the right path; it is like blind leading blind, which is not good. The Bible wastes no time teaching us that bad company corrupts good manners.

Parents, we must pray continuously for our children because, many times, they might be going down the wrong path. A good trait is to sit with them and discuss what is happening in their world and what they might be encountering. Do weekly checkups so they know you care as a parent. They are the future, and the enemy wants to destroy them, so they do not fulfil their purpose.

A New Chapter

I got tired of staying home, so I signed up for The Heart Academy in Portmore, St Catherine, Jamaica. I got accepted to study building technology in 2006. I lived in Clarendon, so I had to stay on the School campus. Boarding was fun as I got a chance to enjoy concerts, play football, go to the shopping mall, meet new friends and family, and attend prayer meetings. Did I say "prayer meeting?" YES! Things were working out for my good, and I started to see things differently, knowing I was getting older each day.

My time at The Heart Academy taught me to be responsible. I had to do my class work and building projects, ensuring they were completed on time. I also built a side wall, which was a part of my good grades. Life in Portmore was not just about having fun. One thing I cannot forget is how hot it was.

The course I was doing was only six (6) months, so as time drew closer, I started to ponder what my next move would be after leaving school and how I could help my grandmother. I never wanted my grandmother to think she had wasted her money on me. I tried to make her proud and show her that I did something good with my life. I aimed to help her to the best of my ability.

1 Corinthians 2:9 - *Eyes hath not seen, nor ear heard, neither have entered into the heart of man the things which God hath prepared for them that love him.*

While I was there wondering, I believe God was smiling, knowing He had something in store for me. When we think all hope is gone, 'Grace' says not so. When we think less of ourselves, the will of God is greater than our human mind can comprehend. The way God sees us is not based on our background, family or what others think or say about us. It is sad to tell, but sometimes, because some people did not achieve what they intended, they believe another person should not achieve it either. The devil is a liar! Stay away from dream killers who think and even speak that you will not make it out of the pit or the valley you are in.

3 John 2:2

Beloved, I wish above all things that thou mayest prosper and be in health, even as thy soul prospereth.

Jeremiah 1:5 - ***Before I formed you in the womb, I knew thee, and before thou camest forth out of the womb, I sanctified thee and ordained thee a prophet unto the nations.***

Let me point out that having a positive mindset and speaking positive words in our lives is also very important. When we think right, it helps us to see right; when we see right, it allows us to talk right. (positive affirmations.) The only one that can stop you is YOU.

I mentioned positive affirmations because while in Portmore, I would watch the airplanes coming down for landing and point in the sky and say, "One day, I will be able to fly in one of those airplanes." I did not understand then that I was speaking and declaring positive affirmations over my life every time I said those words.

One Friday afternoon, on the last day of my courses, my phone rang, and it was my father from the Cayman Islands. He said to me, "Delano! would you love to come to Cayman tomorrow?" I quickly replied, "YES." He then told me to pack my clothes. I left the school in a hurry to get to the bus stop to catch the bus home to May Pen Clarendon. That Friday night, I could not sleep; I was too anxious for daybreak to come.

The day finally came *(October 28, 2006),* and I was going to the airport. I felt so happy to travel in an airplane for the first time. A songwriter put it perfectly when she said, **"When Jesus says yes, nobody can't say no."**

Never give up on life. You never know what the next minute or hour will be for you. I spent a lot of time worrying, and all that time, God was paving the way for me to go to Grand Cayman Island. My grandmother always prayed that my dad would help me someday; however, my father always seemed to face opposition whenever he tried to assist me. But God stepped in right on time. I have learned that when God open doors for you, no man can shut it. The Lord sees and knows everything, even the secret of every man's heart. If I was not a Christian back then and He showed up for me, how much more now that I am saved, sanctified and filled with His Spirit?

Life In The Cayman Islands

On the 30th of October 2006, I started working in the same company with my father as a gardener and a truck driver. I felt good working in the Cayman Islands and having my own money to buy whatever I wanted, and I could afford to go wherever I needed to. One day, my mother said to me, "Lano, save your money because you do not have a chick or a child." I never listened. I was living a fast life.

Proverbs 19:20

Hear counsel, and receive instruction, that thou mayest be wise in thy latter end.
Reader!

I must admit that I did not take wise counsel. Sometimes, God will see you going down the wrong road and speak through someone to stop you before a fall. However, it is up to us to listen. I was disobedient to my mother, so I ended up regretting it.

Ephesian 6:1

Children, obey your parents in the Lord, for this is right.

Proverbs 10:8

The wise in heat will receive commandment: but a prating fool shall fall.

Proverbs 12:15

The way of a fool is right in his own eyes.

My way of thinking was wrong, and I started wasting my money. It was like giving a baby a fourteen-karat gold watch to wear, and they just put it in the toilet, not knowing the cost or the effort one put in to get it. I was earning $800ci per week and had no responsibilities, no wife or children to care for. I was trying to imitate the lifestyle of my coworkers. Shopping, girls, and fame were the hit things for us.

It is hard to move forward when you allow yourself to be carried away by your pride or a group of people who do not have a positive view or set goals in life.

Proverbs13:20

He that walketh with the wise men shall be wise: but a companion of fools shall be destroyed.

I was definitely in the company of fools who were thinking the same way as I was. Sometimes in life, we can put ourselves in groups that we believe are best for us based on our fleshly desires. We occasionally do this to prove to others that we are on top.

Time passed, and I formed a party group. Every weekend, we would be at the nightclub because I was the dancer in the group. I would take over the dance floor and was excited when I heard the girls screaming to see more of me. "Yes", we were rocking the nightclubs and went to several clubs per night, depending on the fun we were having. All my goals and dreams were down the drain at this juncture because my life was taking the wrong turn.

Proverbs 3:35

The wise shall inherit glory, but shame shall be the promotion of fools.

I recall occasionally arriving late at work and becoming rebellious, even to my boss and crew members. My father would get a lot of complaints about my actions and that I was constantly sleeping on the job. I started facing one issue after the next, from owing my rent to having no money and falling into depression. I was carrying a pain no one knew about, and I tried to mask that pain with the things of the world.

One day, as I was preparing for a boat party, my father stopped by to check on me. We started talking, and without realizing, it was nightfall. I changed my mind and did not go to the party. That night, when I went to sleep, I had a dream that changed my life.

2
HOW I GOT SAVED

I dreamt I was standing in a line full of people. There were like a million people in this line, but the sad thing is I was at the end. When I looked to my right, I saw a man looking radiant in white attire, standing in the water. It was the prettiest water I have ever witnessed. He pointed his finger at me and said, "It is your turn." I woke up that night fearful, drinking water like I was about to die, and my heart was beating extremely fast. I was anxious for daybreak to come.

After that incident, I attended the City of Faith Church of God in the Cayman Islands. I remember constantly attending their Bible study and prayer meetings because I knew I was in dire need of help as the devil was still trying to keep me in the world. I thank God for a praying Church. They were right there to support and pray with me along my journey.

We often say when God is ready, He will save us, but we must understand that salvation is a choice. God gives humans free will, and we must accept or reject His gift of salvation. The Holy Spirit is nudging many persons to turn from their sinful lifestyle. He even tries to reach many through dreams and visions, but they choose to follow the devil and his plan that is designed to shift us from our purpose. Meanwhile, the Holy Spirit of God is knocking at our hearts, asking us to open up and let Him in.

If you are reading this and are not saved, I implore you to accept Jesus as your Lord and Saviour.

The Word of God reminds us in Romans 6:23 that the wages of sin is death, but the gift of God is eternal life through Christ Jesus.

If you have decided to accept Jesus as your Lord and Saviour, I want you to repeat the following prayer.

"Dear lord Jesus, I come to you now knowing I am a sinner who needs your forgiveness. I believe that you died for my sins and that God- the Father raised you from the dead. Right now, I ask that you forgive my sins, and I invite you into my heart today to save me, in Jesus' name, Amen."

If you have said this simple prayer from your heart, I believe you have been saved according to **Romans 10:9-10**. I now ask that you find a church rooted in the word of God and believe in the power and manifestation of the Holy Ghost so that you can grow in the things of God.

Reflecting on My Journey

On March 28, 2008, I decided to follow Jesus. Being a young convert felt good. I was zealous for the kingdom of God. I attended bible study and prayer meetings every night and was punctual at Sunday morning services. I had a strong desire to grow in the things of God, and I told myself that I would become a pastor one day. I would preach to the flowers while cutting and watering them at work.

Along my Christian journey, I fell into sin and did things I had no business doing. I was very young in the things of God. I had accepted Jesus and loved the Lord, but my mindset needed to be fully transformed. I was still thinking the way I did when I was in the world.

Romans 12:2

And be not conformed to this world: but be ye transformed by the renewing of your mind, that ye may prove what that good, and acceptable, and perfect, will of God is.

Our minds can only be transformed by the word of God. Being saved is one thing, but changing our mindset is paramount. I want also to add that God is a forgiving God. Therefore, if we mess up and truly repent and turn away from doing wrong, He is faithful to cleanse us from all unrighteousness (1 John 1:9).

God is not like man, who often finds it hard to forgive.

I accepted God's forgiveness, got up, brushed myself off and started a clean slate. I was determined not to focus on the naysayers but on God, who had set me FREE.

Romans 8:1
Therefore, there is no condemnation to them, which are in Christ Jesus.

Romans 8:2
For the law of the spirit of life in Christ Jesus hath made me free from the law of sin and death.

I am sharing my testimony to encourage someone. If you make a mistake while walking with the Lord Jesus Christ and feel like giving up, please don't. God has not given up on you. He is waiting, and there is far more to gain, so finish that race with Jesus. He did it for me and will surely do it for you if you allow Him.

Jeremiah 29:11

For I know the thoughts that I think towards you saith the Lord.

***

Praying For A Wife

Months passed until one day, I started to ponder why good men seem unable to find a good woman. With this thought in mind, I started praying for God to help me find a Christian woman to be my wife, one who loves Him, will stand for righteousness, and is not afraid to tell me the truth when I am wrong. With tears pouring down my face, I prayed to God and poured out the desires of my heart.
I continually went to fasting, Bible studies, and prayer meetings, waiting for God to answer my prayer.

Every time a female approached me, I wondered if that person was the answer to my prayers. Some were nice-looking, but something in my spirit would not allow me to lean on my understanding.
I lost focus for a while because I needed a wife, but I decided to focus on God and allow Him to do the rest. I also heeded my pastor's counsel because I was too anxious and was

getting impatient. Eventually, I regained focus and depended totally on God for a wife.

Nugget:

Never move too fast to do anything because of how you feel.

Faith is not how you feel or anything you think, but it is about trusting and standing on the word of God to be true in your heart, knowing God will come through based on His word.

***

There was a ministry called the Church of God Prophetic Ministry. My mother and my friends loved to visit after leaving our Church. Their worship service was kept way past ours, and I loved that I could dance for the Lord. One day, I went to my pastor because of what I heard from my local Church members as a young convert. They told me that we were not allowed to visit other churches because we might return with evil spirits.

What they told me was not sitting right with me, so I told my pastor that I was leaving the church. She informed me that was okay, but I knew she was unhappy with my decision. I went to her out of respect and wanted to be released from the church's membership the right way. She eventually released me.

After a while, I returned to visit my pastor and the church. They were very happy to see me. I believe that in life, we must respect people's choices and also help them along the way to make the right choices.

Years later, I realized that my pastor was looking out for me as a baby in Christ. However, by the time I learned, I was already a member of the next church. I was playing the drums and serving in God's kingdom.

The Answer To My Prayers

One day, a woman of God visited our church. We made eye contact, and I instantly felt a connection. I started pondering how to introduce myself, knowing I never approached or dated a Christian lady before.

One day, I mustered the courage and started talking to her about her hair. Time passed, and we began to meet each other in the evenings to talk about ourselves, our relationship with God, and other things we had discovered in common.

One Sunday morning, I proposed to her during the Church service. With God's help, I could do it because my heart was beating like a drum; I was extremely nervous.

A few months passed, and then I married the love of my life - Shellian Bucknor-Samuels. She is beautiful inside and out, an angel sent by God in my life, caring, and a special gem. "That's my wife."

The hand of God has been upon us since we met, and we saw his hand of favour, even on our wedding day. We received everything we needed to make our wedding a successful one. We got married on December 05, 2009, and the Lord opened a door for us to spend our honeymoon at a hotel we never had to pay for. All I can say is, “God never fails.” Many believed we spent a lot, but "favour" and faith brought us through.

The Beginning Of Our Lives

Our life together was amazing. At age 23, we welcomed our first child - Joseph Samuels. I was so happy to become a father, and I felt proud. One day, I lifted my son to God and thanked Him for blessing us with a child because the doctor had told my wife that she would not be able to have children. However, God always makes a way. He is a miracle-working God.

***

As we enjoyed the new addition to our nuclear family, I noticed that my wife was acting fearful and overly protective of our son, but I empathized because I knew it was a motherly thing. As a husband, I became worried, not understanding what to say or do to help my wife overcome her fears. Both of us were first-time parents, and it did get tiring and stressful at times, but I had to be strong for my wife. My wife has been a wonderful mother to our children - Joseph and Josian. I have learned that when we seek the help of God, it is amazing how things can work for our Good. I thank God for my family.

Reader!!

Sometimes in life, when we need help, all we have to do is ask. I must agree that we cannot ask everyone for help. The Holy Spirit must direct us in this area because some people want to know your story to tell everybody because they want you to feel or look bad. However, few might be willing to help you find the right solution to your problem, God's way.

When we needed help, we did not ask anyone to help us because of fear. Instead, we cried out to God to help us while staying stuck in the problem day by day. We never really understood the meaning of faith and works.

James 2:17

Even so, faith, if it hath not works, is dead.

We were not living by faith in God. As a husband, I was trying to find an easy way out instead of trusting God to lead us so we could encounter victory. We were both under immense stress, but we put on a good show in front of everyone as if everything was okay. We still went to Church, and sometimes, people would ask if we were alright. We would often tell them we were doing well or say we were blessed and highly favoured.

Many persons are going to Church, to their workplace, or at home silently screaming for "Help, needing peace of mind but not understanding how to. On the other hand, Some allow pride to take control, and they would never ask for help.

Proverbs 3:5-6

Trust in the Lord with all thine heart; lean not to thine own understanding. In all thy ways acknowledge Him, and He shall direct thy paths.

My wife and I would have bad moments when things weren't working well in our marriage. Living in the Cayman Islands was not easy for us financially. Sometimes, we had nothing to eat or give to our son, Joseph. Other times, we did not have pampers for our son, so my wife would have to find a way to keep him warm while I went out and begged my friends for help. Even when I was hungry, I sought food for my family. My wife often asked if I was okay, and I would comfort her with a yes, even though my mind was all over the place, thinking what would be next because I could not repeatedly go to the same person for help.

Some persons might be pondering if Christians go through these things. Well, the answer is yes! However, not everyone experiences the same thing. Everyone faces hard times in life, but that does not mean God is not our helper and that He won't intervene. All things work together for our good. I can testify that God was there at every season of our lives.

***

Months passed, and we still faced problems, so my wife became very frustrated. We would argue, and my wife would say that I was to be blamed for our mishap, and she did not know why she agreed to marry me. She even went as far as saying that she wanted a divorce, and she took off her ring for days at a time. We argued almost daily, and I could no longer take the pressure. I eventually left the house

and went to a supermarket, intending to sleep under a flower in the parking lot.
When I got to the supermarket, the stones would not let me sleep, so I returned home and rested on the floor.

I told my wife that she should go if she wanted to leave. Neither of us was happy, and the devil played us like a video game. We did not realize that it was because we did not understand each other and lacked the knowledge to deal with issues like these.

There were days we worked but could not make two ends meet. Everything around us seemed so dark, and because of circumstances, I wanted to go back to the things of the world, but my heart would not allow me.
I was spiritually, mentally, and emotionally out of alignment, and my world needed help. I was afraid of losing my family, and it seemed everything was falling apart. Our situation continued to spiral until our son returned to Jamaica to stay with his grandmother in Kingston.

I have learned that it is best not to act negatively or say things we do not mean when we are going through a rough time, or the things we sometimes say out of frustration can hurt the ones we love.

My wife and I were fooling ourselves before men, "NOT" God; He knows everything we do and what we are about to do.

All it takes as a Christian is to be truthful to ourselves, knowing that we are not "robots" and that things happen in life, even on this road or path with Jesus Christ. Many persons are sitting in Church services day in and night out, who were only told that everything is going to be okay, which is good, but have never been shown how to handle situations as believers. We must give a listening ear to each other as brothers and sisters in Christ. The truth is, sometimes, we all need someone to talk to.

Often, many persons could help their brothers and sisters in Christ, but they refuse to. God blessed them so they could be a blessing to others, but because of the hardness of their heart, they ignored the conviction of the Holy

Spirit and failed their test. They missed the opportunity to be a vessel of honour that God can use to bless someone else.

The Bible encourages us to be our brothers' keepers; in other words, “Be there for each other.” The truth is, we do not always find those qualities in some churches, and that is why it is very important to have a personal relationship with the Lord Jesus Christ because folks will not always be around to help you.

Psalm 124:8

Our help is in the name of the Lord, who made heaven and Earth.

Psalm125:1

They that trust in the Lord shall be as mount Zion, which cannot be removed but abideth forever.

We sometimes see others looking pretty on the outside but dying on the inside. If it lays on your heart to help a brother or sister in the Lord, "do it" by putting action to your words because the kingdom of God is not just about words.

Act 3:6-7

Then Peter said, "But such as I have I give thee; in the Name of Jesus Christ of Nazareth, rise up and walk. (7) Peter took him by the right hand and lifted him; immediately, his feet and ankle bones received strength.?

Notice!! Peter gave the man the word for his problem and gave him a helping hand to rise up. Let us do the same for the "Glory of God" by helping someone. Never stop doing good to others because you might need someone to return the favour one day.

Never Ending Battles

Time passed, and we were still going through a storm, but who God put together let no man put asunder. We continued to push against all odds, staying true to our vows before God.

We continued serving in ministry, but sad to say, the Church we were attending closed because of lack of support. We had to find a different church. We started attending the New Testament Church of God for a while, and then we became members and joined the choir to help us keep our minds on the things of God.

Going to a different Ministry did not change everything. We were still facing sorrow in areas of our lives, but we kept on serving like everything was okay with us.

One day, I went to my landlord and asked her if I could cut the grass at the home for the money we owed her for rent because we did not have the money to pay her. She said no, and the saddest part is that someone else cut it the following day. We were living in Randyke, George Town, Grand Cayman, then.

The following night, when I finished moderating at the youth event, it was very late, and upon our arrival home, my wife and I realized that we had been locked out of our room by the landlord. I was wet from head to toe and tired. I could not let my wife keep on those clothes, so I found a way to get some clothes for her. I felt so uncomfortable about the situation, knowing I had asked my landlord for an alternative.

At about 11:30 pm, I called a brother in Christ, asking him if we could stay at his home because we had nowhere to go, and he agreed. Our minds were all over the place, wondering, “Where was God in our situation.” I felt like I was on the brink of giving up. I was working but not making enough money to care for my family.

I felt like a fish out of water begging for life, living in a wonderland, wandering away and seeing the pain in my wife's eyes. I sometimes wondered if God did not see what we were going through. It seemed we had problems in every area of our lives. My wife often said, "God, why me?"

***God’s plan for His people is not always visible, but we must have faith during the bad times. God will come through for us no matter what the devil says or does*.**

****

There were days when my wife and I had to stay with other Church families. We would sleep on the floor for weeks because there was

not enough space. Living in poverty was not a nice feeling.
Many nights, we had to decide where to sleep. Some nights, when we got tired of sleeping on the floor, we would sleep on the bus as I was a bus driver. Life has a way of making you feel like a prisoner, even when you try and try.

Sometimes, we must be tested to be developed into the men and women of God that we ought to become and to help others on their journey with our story so that God can get the glory.

Psalm47:7

For God is the king of all the earth, sing ye praise with understanding.

Psalm50:1

The mighty God, even the Lord, hath spoken and called the earth from the rising of the sun unto the going thereof.

***

We were grateful for the help, but things changed because they needed their space. Eventually, we had to leave, even though we had nowhere to go. Of course, we continued going to church but weren't being edified because our minds were so distracted by the issues in our lives. I often wanted to give up on God but could not because something would always tell me, "Keep on going. Just a little bit longer." We were longing for a breakthrough in our life "expeditiously". Well, you know what they say: no test, no testimony.

Nuggets:
Out of pain can come success, but only if you want it to amidst not knowing; always lean to the one who can bring you through.

If the devil can get to our minds, then he got us. Our mind is an essential part of our being and a battlefield in the spirit realm. We must keep our minds pure, thinking and using the word of God daily because sometimes sinful thoughts come to our minds as Christians.

Therefore, it is very important to live a repentant life.
No matter how long one is a Christian or how much we think we know, sinful thoughts will come because there is a devil who wants to see us fail, but keep pressing because there is a victory to be won. The word of God is the number one factor in renewing our minds.

Romans12:2
And be not conformed to this world: but be transformed by renewing your mind.

For us to start doing things differently in our lives, it must begin with our mind being renewed because the way of the Lord is the best, whether we like it or not.

Proverbs 24:9
The thought of foolishness is sin, and the scorner is an abomination to men.

Foolish thoughts have nothing to do with God. He gets no Glory from it. It is best always to think positively, even when it is difficult. I say this because I can relate.

One day, I was out trying to see what I could do to make some money. I was driving a public bus from George Town to West Bay, but nothing seemed to work out. I went to the Christian store to buy a Jesus sticker to put on the bus for the passengers to read, and a man came behind me in the line and said to me, "Nice sticker." I told him, “Thank you, sir.” When I finished cashing, I went outside, and he stopped me and said, “Can I ask you a question?”

Reader!

God has a way of doing things we cannot even begin to imagine.

1 Peter 5:7 - Casting all your care upon him; for He careth for you.

We may often think God does not care because we face many problems and are not getting the desired results. Sometimes, we are at fault, pushing back the hand of God by trying to do things on our own. When we think it is all over, God will show up; even through a conversation, He can prove that He has not forgotten us. God never fails.

<u>Psalm 46:1</u>

God is our refuge and strength, a very present help in trouble.

The man that I met at the Christian store asked me to bring some people for him to Church. I thought he already had the people for me to carry, so I expected to be paid. With that in mind, I quickly told him yes. I later found out that I was the one he was hoping to find the people and bring them to his Ministry. I was so desperate, and that caused me to say yes without understanding what was being asked of me.

My wife and I visited his ministry, Honor and Glory, the following day. It was about 3 pm. Not many of us were there, but the message was great. He talked about the Blood of Jesus. This happened in 2012 in September.
Let us understand one thing: it is not about the crowd but the Spirit of God, which makes a difference in the lives of His people for His glory.

The Pastor, Clayton McGhie, allowed the Spirit of God to lead him.

After service was over and everyone finished talking and greeting each other, the Pastor asked my wife and me what we were going home to eat. My wife and I looked at each other, and I told him nothing. Right there, God showed up for us, allowing Pastor Clayton and his wife to bring us to a nice Chinese restaurant to dine with them and talk.

My friends, God will always make way for us, no matter how it seems to us at times.

***

While talking at the restaurant, they asked us to get some clothes and come over to their home on Monday to stay for a while so we could get to know each other better. I started wondering if I was dreaming. My wife and I planned to move out on Wednesday of the same week, having nothing.

Monday morning came, and we went to their house according to plan. We were given our room with a nice AC system and carpet floor. My wife and I slept like a baby. We could hardly wake up that morning to go to work.

Eventually, we made up our minds to be a member of his ministry. They took us under their wings to teach us and helped our marriage to be the marriage that God intended it to be. They counseled us God's way. It was now up to my wife and I to apply what we were taught.

God worked things out for us. Just when we thought it was over, He showed up on time. We thank the Lord for what He has done through these people of God.

Proverbs 3:13 - Happy is the man that finds wisdom and the man that gets understanding.

Days passed, and it reached the point where the pastor had to travel to the United States. Each day, he would go on the road looking for a place for us to stay; no more running around like a "chicken without a head." They also continued to impart wisdom concerning the things of God as sons and daughters.

It was not easy for us because we always depended on our ability. We had to change our mindset and study the word of God consistently, which was a big problem because we were distracted for so long.

Many of us know the Bible word for word, from Genesis to Revelation, which is good, but that is not all that is required. We must allow our lives to demonstrate the word of God by letting it become a part of us daily. This is unnecessary to prove anything, but the unsaved will see how we live and be drawn to our Lord Jesus as their Saviour.
Our conduct plays a very important role in the world because, as believers, we are like a mirror to the world. Jesus said that we are the light of the world.

St John 3:16 - For God loved the world so much that he gave his one and only son so that whoever believes in Him may not be lost but have eternal life.

So, after we became full-time members, we started to fix up the location. We were having Church every Sunday. Serving is a good thing even when we do not feel like it. We must understand that feelings on this Christian journey often cause us to miss God's Blessing.

Our feelings cannot be trusted. As a believer in Jesus Christ, it is important to be led by the Spirit of God rather than our emotions.

My wife and I served in ministry not to look good but for God's Glory, knowing that faithfulness will pay off one day. We served even when things were broken in our lives, when we were without a job, when our child needed to be taken care of, and when bills needed to be paid. We continued because we knew that God had been there for us, failing not.

If you are serving in ministry, let your serving be unto God because He will reward you in due season. Do not give up even amid "Church hurt" (which I also encountered).

As Christians, we must remember that we are living in a real world with real things that happen, but being Church hurt was not a good thing for me Physically and Spiritually. I could not worship or pray as I used to because crying was my thing, knowing that the emotional wound that was inflicted was coming from leaders I looked up to. Many times, I wanted to run away. I thought about it over and over.

It's not wise to try to run from our pain because it will keep coming. Emotional hurt is internal, and "yes" fear can cause us not to deal with what is stopping us from going forward.

I decided to face my fear, not by my ability but with the Lord's help. We need not allow the hurt to cause us to shut God out of our hearts.

Psalm12:1- Help, lord; for the godly man ceaseth, for the faithful fail from among the children of men.

I faced my fear while looking back at where God had taken me from and how He was present in good and bad times. I also listened to positive stuff that encouraged me in my walk with God so I could stand again in faith, forgive those who hurt me, and forgive myself.

One day, I was at the gas station pumping air into the bus tyre, and one of the leaders who hurt me saw me and walked over to me. I hugged the person, and the individual hugged me as well. After that, we both smiled.

Forgiveness is key when hurt, especially by the ones we love. I am not saying it will be easy, but it is the right thing to do to prevent us from blocking our blessings.

1 John 2:10 - ***He that loveth his brother abideth in the light, and there is none occasion of stumbling in him.***

When the Devil sees something Good in us, he will try to do everything to stop us from fulfilling our God-given purpose. I want to remind you that you have a purpose to fulfill for God's Glory.
God surely has a way of bringing us through training before He appoints us. I am reminded of the story of David as a little boy caring for his father's sheep. Maybe he wanted to give up because he was the only onc doing everything. His brothers did not help, but he did his duty, not realizing God was bringing him through the training as an upcoming king over Israel. During David's time in the desert, a lion and a bear appeared, and David and the

sheep were in danger. God empowered him to kill the bear and lion and protect the sheep.
I believe David did not know that he was going to war with Goliath or become a king, nor did his family. They only saw David as a shepherd boy. The revelation in the text is that the lion represents Goliath's strength, the Bear represents his height, and the sheep represent Israel - God's people. When David was about to fight Goliath, he told King Saul about his victory, and he defeated Goliath.

Reader
Before God can promote us, he has a way of testing the reigns of our hearts. Several other persons in the Bible were tested before they were elevated.

Psalm 46:1 - God is our refuge and strength, a very present help in trouble.

Never forget that God, the creator of heaven and earth, will never fail us, no matter what we go through. He can do exceedingly and abundantly all that we can ever ask or think about. Let us be of good courage, having hope in the lord.

I have been through so much in my life, like the story of David. My family and even myself never saw the true purpose of God inside me. I sometimes felt like giving up and throwing in the towel when going through my ups and downs. I was walking in pride several times and failing a lot of tests. When I was attending High School, a teacher once told me I would never excel. I remember feeling hopeless and like an outcast, but God kept me through the darkest parts of my life. When many gave up on me, He never gave up on me. Thank you, Jesus!

God have used great men and women of God to help birth purpose in me. All those who looked down on me now have to be looking up to me, all for the glory of God. When Jesus says 'YES", nobody can say "NO."
I live my life for the Lord Jesus Christ, giving him all Glory and Honor because He deserves it all. He transformed my life and blessed me with a family. If God did it for me, He can do it for you; trust Him.

Deuteronomy 31:6 - Be strong and courageous. Do not fear or be in dread of

them, for it is the LORD your God who goes with you.

***

God will not leave you nor forsake you.

3

MY LIFE AS A MINISTER

One Sunday morning in 2013, I was asked to wear black and white to church. I never knew it was my elevation to the post of Minister of the Gospel. I never believed I would become a Minister for Jesus Christ.

Being a minister was not easy because I still faced problems. I cried many times. People might think that when a person becomes a minister, they no longer face problems, but that is far from the truth. We are tested with good or bad daily, even as ministers. Many times, I felt so low in my spirit and discouraged. Yes! Things like these will happen because we are humans "NOT" robots. Whenever we find ourselves in this position as a Child of God, we must learn to encourage ourselves and have faith.

Psalm 121:1 - ***I will lift my eyes unto the hills from whence cometh my help. My help cometh from the lord, which made heaven and earth.***

Believe it or not, we must know where our true help comes from when facing difficulty.

***

Time went by, and my wife left for Jamaica. As a man of God, I can remember sleeping on the church floor many times, not because of any special event but because I did not have a place to live. Sometimes, I would sleep on the altar, and other times on the chairs to sleep well. I often had to hide from the members because I did not know who to trust. The laws differed in the Cayman Islands from those in my native country.

Sometimes, I needed to bathe, and I waited until everyone left Church. When I was hungry, I would go to a restaurant to beg for food each day. Once again, God helped me and turned things around. Thank you, Jesus, for loving me. Sometimes, when we think we are alone, we are not.

Not everyone will understand what you are going through as a Minister because they think you should have it all nice with a lot of money, too. People will often change and turn their back on you when you need them, but God will never change. He is the same yesterday, today and forever.

Elevation During My Chaos

Two years after being appointed as a minister, I was ordained again in 2015. It was a great moment to see myself among the Great leaders of the Gospel of Jesus Christ and receive my Certificate again.

I owe all praises to Jesus Christ. My life was like a book with blank pages, just going through the motions, hoping to see a change one day. I did not know what to do as a young man in my twenties. It's like a boy was crying out for help inside me, wondering who would listen to my cry for help. But God!

As an Evangelist, I tried to reach out to many souls for the kingdom of God. Some embarrassed me when I told them about Jesus Christ, while some asked if I had an education and shouted at me to leave their house. The truth is, I felt bad and sometimes wanted to stop, but the spirit of God reminded me of His word.

Matthew 10:14- *If anyone will not welcome you or listen to your words, leave that home or town, and shake the dust off your feet.*

I kept on sharing the Gospel even to this day.
As ambassadors for Christ, we must understand who called us into the body of Christ and do the good work of Him that sent us. He is the author and finisher of our faith. Jesus is returning with a reward to pay every man according to their work on earth. Therefore, let us go forward for Jesus, telling the world about His true love and forgiveness. Let us work together to build the kingdom of God.

I may not have it all together, but I continually share the Gospel of Jesus Christ. We might not always get everything together, but we must trust the Lord's hand to keep moulding us, breaking us and fashioning us for His Glory. What is life without Christ? Empty!

Jeremiah 18:6 - ***Can I not, O house of Israel, deal with you as this potter does?" declares the Lord. "Behold, like the clay in the potter's hand, so are you in My hand, O house of Israel.***

4

BECOMING A PASTOR

As an Evangelist, God was always watching my faithfulness towards Him. Within three (3) years, on the 8th of April 2018, I was ordained again as a "Pastor" of Honor and Glory International Christian Center. I thank God for this Ministry that He used to help me give birth to purpose. God also opened the door of favour for my wife to return to the Cayman Islands. She was also ordained as an Evangelist. I never knew this day would come, my God! It was nothing but God's grace and mercy.

Let us never write people off; rather, let us ask God to help us identify the calling on their life and to give us the ability to help them give birth to it.

As a Pastor, the work of God never stops. Some people think it does, but when you become a pastor, the ministry work never ends. Sometimes, I felt tired, hungry, and discouraged, but I did the work. I thank God for the great leaders who served along the way in ministry, making my work less tedious so that I could do other things I needed to.

As a Pastor, one must never try to do everything because they will be burnt out. We must trust other leaders to work in their father's kingdom, knowing that we can never accomplish the goals set before us by ourselves.

Reader:

When man says you are nothing, God says you are something. Look at me now, "Pastor Delano Samuels." Glory to God! Purpose never dies, and the Prophetic word never lies. All we need to do is stay in line with God and go through our seasons, as they help prepare us for the calling on our life.

God will not always give us the answer to the puzzle. I can relate because I never understood why I was going through what I went through. It all makes sense now that I am a pastor and writing my book. **Where would I be if the Lord was not on my side**? I made it to this point in my life because of Him. Truly, this "Unknown journey of my life has manifested, so again, I say, "Glory to my Lord and Savior Jesus Christ."

Jeremiah 29:11 - ***For I know the plans I have for you; declares the Lord, plans to prosper you and not to harm you, plans to give you hope and future.***

your
on Jesus

THE GRACE OF GOD CAN KEEP YOU WHEREVER YOU GO IN THIS LIFE. NEVER FORGET THAT YOU ARE VALUABLE TO GOD.

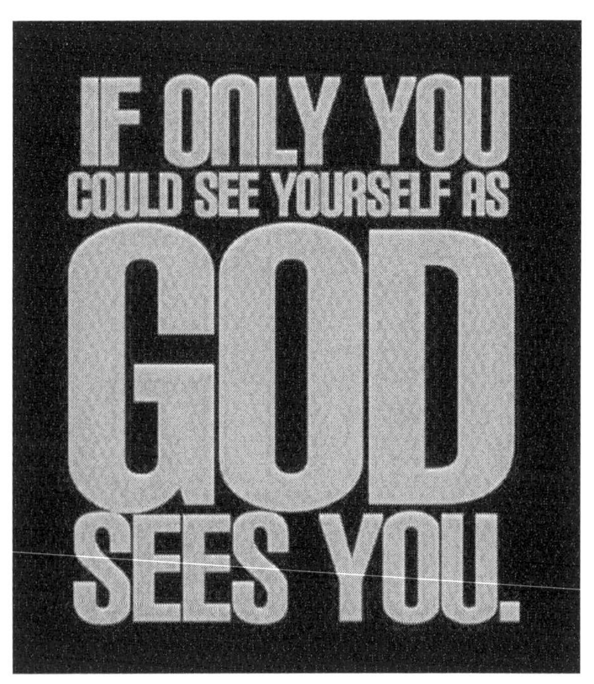

Our Children Joseph Samuels And Josian Samuels. The Lord Bless them and keep them, in Jesus' Name.

SUPER

Renew The Mind; Get Better Results!

Scriptures to study

- ✓ **Romans 12:1-2** - I appeal to you therefore, brothers, by the mercies of God, to present your bodies as a living sacrifice, holy and acceptable to God, which is your spiritual worship. Do not be conformed to this world, but be transformed by the renewal of your mind, that by testing, you may discern what is the will of God, what is good and acceptable and perfect.

- ✓ **Ephesians 4:22-24** - Put off your old self, which belongs to your former manner of life and is corrupt through deceitful desires, and be renewed in the spirit of your minds, and to put on the new self, created after the likeness of God in true righteousness and holiness.

- ✓ **Colossians 3:10** - And have put on the new self, which is being renewed in knowledge in the image of its Creator."

- ✓ **Philippians 4:8** - Finally, brothers, whatever is true, whatever is honourable, whatever is just, whatever is pure, whatever is lovely, whatever is commendable, if there is any excellence, if there is anything worthy of praise, think about these things.

- ✓ Colossians 3:2-3 "Set your minds on things above, not on earthly things. [3] For you died, and your life is now hidden with Christ in God.

- ✓ **2 Corinthians 4:16-18** "So we do not lose heart. Though our outer self is wasting away, our inner self is being renewed daily. For this light momentary affliction is preparing for us an eternal weight of glory beyond all comparison, as we look not to the things that are seen but to the things that are unseen. For the things that are seen are transient, but the things that are unseen are eternal.

- ✓ **Romans 7:25** - Thanks be to God through Jesus Christ our Lord! So then, I myself serve the law of God with my mind, but with my flesh, I serve the law of sin.

Keep Your Mind on Christ

Philippians 4:6-7 - Do not be anxious about anything, but in everything by prayer and supplication with thanksgiving let your requests be made known to God. And the peace of God, which surpasses all understanding, will guard your hearts and minds in Christ Jesus.

ENCYCLOPEDIA
SCIENCE & TECHNO
UNIVERSE

ABOUT THE AUTHOR

Pastor Delano Samuels is a native of Jamaica who resides in the Cayman Islands. From a young age, purpose was instilled in him by his mother, Marcia Samuels, and his father, Jeffrey Samuels.

He attended Central High School in May Pen, where he graduated and pursued further building drawing and construction studies at the Portmore Heart Academy. There, he earned a Level 1 certificate. Committed to advancing his knowledge, He also obtained certifications in AED/CPR and first aid, handyman skills, physical education coaching, and an introduction to business management.

His faith journey led him to embrace salvation through Jesus Christ by faith on March 28, 2008. The following year, on December 5, 2009, he was blessed to marry his darling wife, Shellian Samuels, who has been a tower of strength and a true blessing in his life. They have been graced with two wonderful children, Josian and Joseph Samuels, who bring endless joy and fulfilment to their family.

Pastor Delano was ordained as a pastor on the 8th of April 2018. His dedication to serving in the kingdom of God allowed him to be further ordained as a Reverend Minister by the International Council of Clergy in the USA on January 6, 2023.

Divine Book Design
& Consultants

Made in the USA
Columbia, SC
24 December 2024

48402724R00054